Ballet Memory Journal: The Nutcracker

By: Sunflower Design Publishing

My Memories Dancing

For many ballerinas around the world, The Nutcracker, is an annual tradition. The purpose of this journal is to record your audition information, roles danced, practice notes, and fun holiday memories while performing The Nutcracker.

This journal includes 15 years of Nutcracker performances.

Contents:

Photo or drawing pages

Organizational Pages: Audition, Performance Notes, Choreographer, Technique, & Costume Notes

15 Short Term (ex: a goal during the current Nutcracker Season) & 15 Long Term Goal Pages (ex: an annual goal to work towards for the next audition etc…)

Dedication Pages: An opportunity to reflect upon the work documented in this journal and to aspire towards the future.

This journal is for you.

Enjoy!

Audition date:

_____

Choreographer:

_____

_____

Role(s):

_____

_____

_____

Performance Notes:

_____

_____

_____

_____

_____

_____

_____

_____

_____

_____

_____

_____

_____

Technique Notes:

_____

_____

_____

_____

_____

_____

_____

_____

_____

Costume Notes:

_____

_____

_____

_____

_____

_____

_____

_____

Memories:

_____

_____

_____

_____

_____

_____

_____

_____

_____

_____

_____

_____

_____

_____

_____

_____

_____

_____

Short Term Goal

My short term goal is to…

_____

_____

_____

_____

_____

_____

I will achieve this goal by:

_____

_____

_____

_____

My Reward is:

_____

_____

_____

_____

_____

_____

_____

Long Term Goal

My long term goal is to...

_____

_____

_____

_____

_____

I will achieve this goal by:

_____

_____

_____

My Reward is:

_____

_____

_____

_____

_____

Audition date:

Choreographer:

Role(s):

Performance Notes:

Technique Notes:

_____

_____

_____

_____

_____

_____

_____

_____

_____

Costume Notes:

_____

_____

_____

_____

_____

_____

_____

_____

Memories:

_____

_____

_____

_____

_____

_____

_____

_____

_____

_____

_____

_____

_____

_____

_____

_____

_____

_____

_____

Short Term Goal

My short term goal is to...

_____

_____

_____

_____

I will achieve this goal by:

_____

_____

_____

My Reward is:

_____

_____

_____

_____

_____

Long Term Goal

My long term goal is to…

_____

_____

_____

_____

_____

I will achieve this goal by:

_____

_____

_____

_____

My Reward is:

_____

_____

_____

_____

_____

Audition date:

Choreographer:

Role(s):

Performance Notes:

Technique Notes:

_____

_____

_____

_____

_____

_____

_____

_____

_____

Costume Notes:

_____

_____

_____

_____

_____

_____

_____

_____

Memories:

_____

_____

_____

_____

_____

_____

_____

_____

_____

_____

_____

_____

_____

_____

_____

_____

_____

_____

My short term goal is to...

_____

_____

_____

_____

_____

I will achieve this goal by:

_____

_____

_____

My Reward is:

_____

_____

_____

_____

_____

_____

_____

Long Term Goal

My long term goal is to…

_____

_____

_____

_____

I will achieve this goal by:

_____

_____

_____

My Reward is:

_____

_____

_____

_____

_____

Audition date:

Choreographer:

Role(s):

Performance Notes:

Technique Notes:

_____

_____

_____

_____

_____

_____

_____

_____

Costume Notes:

_____

_____

_____

_____

_____

_____

_____

Memories:

Short Term Goal

My short term goal is to…

_____

_____

_____

_____

_____

I will achieve this goal by:

_____

_____

_____

_____

My Reward is:

_____

_____

_____

_____

_____

_____

Long Term Goal

My long term goal is to...

_____

_____

_____

_____

_____

I will achieve this goal by:

_____

_____

_____

_____

My Reward is:

_____

_____

_____

_____

_____

_____

Audition date:

_____

Choreographer:

_____

_____

Role(s):

_____

_____

_____

Performance Notes:

_____

_____

_____

_____

_____

_____

_____

_____

_____

_____

_____

_____

_____

Technique Notes:

_____

_____

_____

_____

_____

_____

_____

_____

_____

Costume Notes:

_____

_____

_____

_____

_____

_____

_____

_____

Memories:

Short Term Goal

My short term goal is to…

_____

_____

_____

_____

_____

I will achieve this goal by:

_____

_____

_____

_____

My Reward is:

_____

_____

_____

_____

_____

_____

_____

Long Term Goal

My long term goal is to…

_____

_____

_____

_____

_____

I will achieve this goal by:

_____

_____

_____

_____

My Reward is:

_____

_____

_____

_____

_____

_____

Audition date:

Choreographer:

Role(s):

Performance Notes:

Technique Notes:

_____

_____

_____

_____

_____

_____

_____

_____

_____

_____

Costume Notes:

_____

_____

_____

_____

_____

_____

_____

_____

_____

Memories:

_____

_____

_____

_____

_____

_____

_____

_____

_____

_____

_____

_____

_____

_____

_____

_____

_____

_____

Short Term Goal

My short term goal is to…

_____

_____

_____

_____

_____

I will achieve this goal by:

_____

_____

_____

My Reward is:

_____

_____

_____

_____

_____

_____

Long Term Goal

My long term goal is to…

_____

_____

_____

_____

_____

I will achieve this goal by:

_____

_____

_____

_____

My Reward is:

_____

_____

_____

_____

_____

Audition date:

Choreographer:

Role(s):

Performance Notes:

Technique Notes:

_____

_____

_____

_____

_____

_____

_____

_____

_____

Costume Notes:

_____

_____

_____

_____

_____

_____

_____

_____

Memories:

_____

_____

_____

_____

_____

_____

_____

_____

_____

_____

_____

_____

_____

_____

_____

_____

_____

Short Term Goal

My short term goal is to...

_____

_____

_____

_____

_____

I will achieve this goal by:

_____

_____

_____

_____

My Reward is:

_____

_____

_____

_____

_____

_____

Long
Term Goal

My long term goal is to…

_____

_____

_____

_____

_____

I will achieve this goal by:

_____

_____

_____

My Reward is:

_____

_____

_____

_____

_____

Audition date:

Choreographer:

Role(s):

Performance Notes:

Technique Notes:

_____

_____

_____

_____

_____

_____

_____

_____

_____

Costume Notes:

_____

_____

_____

_____

_____

_____

_____

_____

Memories:

_____

_____

_____

_____

_____

_____

_____

_____

_____

_____

_____

_____

_____

_____

_____

_____

_____

_____

My short term goal is to…

_____

_____

_____

_____

_____

I will achieve this goal by:

_____

_____

_____

_____

My Reward is:

_____

_____

_____

_____

_____

_____

Long Term Goal

My long term goal is to…

_____

_____

_____

_____

_____

I will achieve this goal by:

_____

_____

_____

_____

My Reward is:

_____

_____

_____

_____

_____

Audition date:

Choreographer:

Role(s):

Performance Notes:

Technique Notes:

_____

_____

_____

_____

_____

_____

_____

_____

_____

_____

Costume Notes:

_____

_____

_____

_____

_____

_____

_____

_____

_____

Memories:

Short Term Goal

My short term goal is to…

_____

_____

_____

_____

_____

I will achieve this goal by:

_____

_____

_____

_____

My Reward is:

_____

_____

_____

_____

_____

_____

Long Term Goal

My long term goal is to…

_____

_____

_____

_____

_____

I will achieve this goal by:

_____

_____

_____

My Reward is:

_____

_____

_____

_____

_____

Audition date:

_____

Choreographer:

_____

_____

Role(s):

_____

_____

_____

Performance Notes:

_____

_____

_____

_____

_____

_____

_____

_____

_____

_____

_____

_____

Technique Notes:

_____

_____

_____

_____

_____

_____

_____

_____

Costume Notes:

_____

_____

_____

_____

_____

_____

_____

Memories:

Short Term Goal

My short term goal is to…

_____

_____

_____

_____

_____

I will achieve this goal by:

_____

_____

_____

My Reward is:

_____

_____

_____

_____

_____

_____

Long Term Goal

My long term goal is to…

_____

_____

_____

_____

_____

_____

I will achieve this goal by:

_____

_____

_____

_____

My Reward is:

_____

_____

_____

_____

_____

Audition date:

_____

Choreographer:

_____

_____

Role(s):

_____

_____

_____

Performance Notes:

_____

_____

_____

_____

_____

_____

_____

_____

_____

_____

_____

_____

Technique Notes:

_____

_____

_____

_____

_____

_____

_____

_____

_____

Costume Notes:

_____

_____

_____

_____

_____

_____

_____

_____

Memories:

_____

_____

_____

_____

_____

_____

_____

_____

_____

_____

_____

_____

_____

_____

_____

_____

_____

_____

Short
Term Goal

My short term goal is to…

_____

_____

_____

_____

_____

I will achieve this goal by:

_____

_____

_____

My Reward is:

_____

_____

_____

_____

_____

_____

Long Term Goal

My long term goal is to…

_____

_____

_____

_____

_____

_____

I will achieve this goal by:

_____

_____

_____

_____

My Reward is:

_____

_____

_____

_____

_____

_____

Audition date:

_____

Choreographer:

_____

_____

Role(s):

_____

_____

_____

Performance Notes:

_____

_____

_____

_____

_____

_____

_____

_____

_____

_____

_____

_____

_____

_____

Technique Notes:

_____

_____

_____

_____

_____

_____

_____

_____

Costume Notes:

_____

_____

_____

_____

_____

_____

_____

_____

Memories:

_____

_____

_____

_____

_____

_____

_____

_____

_____

_____

_____

_____

_____

_____

_____

_____

_____

_____

_____

_____

Short Term Goal

My short term goal is to…

_____

_____

_____

_____

_____

I will achieve this goal by:

_____

_____

_____

My Reward is:

_____

_____

_____

_____

_____

_____

Long Term Goal

My long term goal is to…

_____

_____

_____

_____

_____

_____

I will achieve this goal by:

_____

_____

_____

_____

My Reward is:

_____

_____

_____

_____

_____

_____

Audition date:

_____

Choreographer:

_____

_____

Role(s):

_____

_____

Performance Notes:

_____

_____

_____

_____

_____

_____

_____

_____

_____

_____

_____

Technique Notes:

Costume Notes:

Memories:

_____

_____

_____

_____

_____

_____

_____

_____

_____

_____

_____

_____

_____

_____

_____

_____

_____

_____

Short Term Goal

My short term goal is to…

_____

_____

_____

_____

_____

I will achieve this goal by:

_____

_____

_____

My Reward is:

_____

_____

_____

_____

_____

_____

_____

Long Term Goal

My long term goal is to…

_____

_____

_____

_____

_____

I will achieve this goal by:

_____

_____

_____

My Reward is:

_____

_____

_____

_____

_____

Audition date:

_____

Choreographer:

_____

_____

Role(s):

_____

_____

_____

Performance Notes:

_____

_____

_____

_____

_____

_____

_____

_____

_____

_____

_____

_____

_____

Technique Notes:

_____

_____

_____

_____

_____

_____

_____

_____

Costume Notes:

_____

_____

_____

_____

_____

_____

_____

Memories:

_____

_____

_____

_____

_____

_____

_____

_____

_____

_____

_____

_____

_____

_____

_____

_____

_____

_____

_____

Short Term Goal

My short term goal is to…

_____

_____

_____

_____

_____

I will achieve this goal by:

_____

_____

_____

_____

My Reward is:

_____

_____

_____

_____

_____

_____

Long
Term Goal

My long term goal is to…

_____

_____

_____

_____

_____

_____

I will achieve this goal by:

_____

_____

_____

_____

My Reward is:

_____

_____

_____

_____

_____

Audition date:

_____

Choreographer:

_____

_____

Role(s):

_____

_____

_____

Performance Notes:

_____

_____

_____

_____

_____

_____

_____

_____

_____

_____

_____

_____

_____

Technique Notes:

_____

_____

_____

_____

_____

_____

_____

_____

_____

Costume Notes:

_____

_____

_____

_____

_____

_____

_____

_____

Memories:

_____

_____

_____

_____

_____

_____

_____

_____

_____

_____

_____

_____

_____

_____

_____

_____

_____

_____

Short Term Goal

My short term goal is to…

_____

_____

_____

_____

_____

I will achieve this goal by:

_____

_____

_____

My Reward is:

_____

_____

_____

_____

_____

_____

Long
Term Goal

My long term goal is to…

_____

_____

_____

_____

_____

I will achieve this goal by:

_____

_____

_____

My Reward is:

_____

_____

_____

_____

_____

_____

I dedicate my work to....

_____

_____

_____

_____

_____

_____

_____

_____

_____

_____

_____

_____

_____

_____

_____

_____

Made in the USA
Middletown, DE
20 November 2019